W9-CAF-518

The
DIRTY SIDE
of the
STORM

ALSO BY MARTHA SERPAS

Côte Blanche

The
DIRTY SIDE
of the
STORM

Martha Serpas

W. W. NORTON & COMPANY

New York • London

For information about permission to reproduce selections from this book,
write to Permissions, W. W. Norton & Company, Inc.,
500 Fifth Avenue, New York, NY 10110

Manufacturing by The Courier Companies, Inc.
Book design by Charlotte Staub
Production manager: Amanda Morrison

Library of Congress Cataloging-in-Publication Data

Serpas, Martha.
The dirty side of the storm / Martha Serpas. — 1st ed.
p. cm.
ISBN-13: 978-0-393-06266-3 (hardcover)
ISBN-10: 0-393-06266-X (hardcover)
1. Louisiana—Poetry. I. Title.
PS3619.E77D57 2007
811'.6—dc22
2006011077

W. W. Norton & Company, Inc.
500 Fifth Avenue, New York, N.Y. 10110
www.wwnorton.com

W. W. Norton & Company Ltd.
Castle House, 75/76 Wells Street, London W1T 3QT

1 2 3 4 5 6 7 8 9 0

FOR
Audrey

CONTENTS

ACKNOWLEDGMENTS

I AM GRATEFUL to the editors of the following publications in which versions of these poems first appeared:

Birmingham Poetry Review: "To the Landlady"
The Christian Century: "Poem Found"
The Connecticut Review: "The Boat Shed," "A Future with Hope," and "No-Name Storm"
Image: A Journal of the Arts and Religion: "Witness Tree," "Reburial at Sea," "The Dirty Side of the Storm," and "Creation"
Kalliope: "An Act of Mercy"
Metre: "Bully Camp Road" and "Ghost Trees"
Passages North: "The Discipline of Nonfulfillment," "Bayou Lafourche," "Sunrise," and "Hard Rain"
Reflections: "The Pomegranate"
Southwest Review: "Fais Do-Do"
The New Yorker: "A Corollary," "Psalm at High Tide," and "The Water"
2River View: "Formica" and "Millennial Birthday"

"Faith in Florida" appeared in the anthology *Vespers: Contemporary American Poems of Religion and Spirituality*

"Poem Found," "Psalm at High Tide," and "Witness Tree" were reprinted in *American Religious Poetry* (Library of America)

My appreciation goes to the Arts Council of Hillsborough County, the Florida State Division of Cultural Affairs, and the University of Tampa, where I am fortunate to teach with exemplary scholars and artists in the English Department. Two nurturing communities, the Yale Institute of Sacred Music and the Yale Divinity School, are sources of ongoing encouragement. I am grateful for the material and visionary assistance of the dedicated people at the Barataria-Terrebonne National Estuary Program; for the wisdom and care of my editor, Angela Vonderlippe; and for the early support of Alice Quinn. Thanks also go to Elizabeth Coffman, Pamela Diamond, Rochelle St. Marie, my research assistant Joel Hanisek, and a number of careful readers: Lisa Birnbaum, Richard Mathews, Don Morrill, Susan Olson, Bettie Perez, Libba Winston, and especially Dahn Dean Gandell, for her sustaining presence. Above all, I am grateful for Hershey and for the constants in my home and heart.

The origins of the poems in this volume preceded Hurricane Katrina's landing in Plaquemines Parish on August 29, 2005, except "Poem Found," written in response to the subsequent levee breaches in New Orleans. Most of the book is set in the Barataria-Terrebonne Estuary (Lafourche and Terrebonne Parishes), Louisiana.

— *MRS*

The
DIRTY SIDE
of the
STORM

Witness Tree

To the right of the altar, Jeanne d'Arc, shorn and shielded,
And very much alive. How surprised I would have been,

As a child, to see her lashed to tree branches instead of
Wielding her blade over the front pews, over Mary's votive

Stand—Mary, determined and confident, her parted cloak
Sheltering the roses and beads of the vulnerable.

Now when the priest's lips press against the marble altar,
I see how we love blood spilled best—what moves in us

We mistrust—corrupted flesh confirms our
Deepest knowledge, our mouths aching

For the relics we become. In the forest's cathedral
The firs refuse to still, pulsing on the hillside,

Chanting even as the brush below them smolders
And the fields settle into a deep red-brown.

How small the bloodshed must look to the witness tree,
From its vantage on the ridge—its maroon

Stripes, only paint warning loggers away. Still it notes
Every gesture in its rings, tastes acrid smoke

From the fires below, recognizes the faces in the fields,
Dogs that chase elk, those that lie down in the dust

And are welcomed on some other hill it alone sees.
Vision without sacrifice, the tree that cannot be felled,

Stronger and greener, that breathes in death and joy
With disinterest and breathes out life and more life.

The Water

In the morning the water like a deckhand,
a persistent curl against the shore,

who won't back down, take no or be denied.
It is there under the wharf and soon under

the house, whoring with any swamp rat
or snake. It rings cypress knees with pearls—

it dreams under the sun like cut cane,
throwing back the salt you wash away,

then wearing pilings down to air.
Your houses wade on stilts tall as pillars,

their sheet metal skulls bared to a mildewed
sky. Against the fallen trees rain and lapping

tide meet, slapping of nets and fish and
naked children pulling driftwood boats

in one joyful noise around your sleep.
In the afternoon the water is there, only more,

browner and grayer, no sweeping seaweed or foam,
just its presence farther up your shore,

like a dull brother-in-law in front of TV.
He means something to somebody—

but not you, not just now. Its slow wake seems
harmless, the litany of waves before a storm

rolling benignly ashore. Intoxicating!
And then it is there, all gray length of it,

rich sex of it, it wants you so badly,
it pounds at the door, *let me take*

your smallness, your jetties, your broad
coasts, your loam. It gathers

at night beyond the curtain of mosquitoes,
darker than the shut-down sky,

the boarded-up clouds. Its desire
thrums like an idling outboard. Ignore

it and it tows itself into your dreams. It's
everywhere, every chance, all the time.

It is more certain than death or love.
It must have been conceived by death and love.

When the last silt sinks under your feet,
you will have to walk out on this water.

A Corollary

Someone, you finally realize, has suffered
your exact misfortune before you.

This one the steady vanishing
of your birthplace before your eyes.

As common and disordered
as a parent burying a child.

You stare down the slate-dark hole again—
this time seeing the blue swirls of precursors

grieving at a murky bottom.
One shouldn't outlive one's birthright:

instead, after you, the feed store boarded,
shorn subdivisions advancing,

your grandchildren pulling their own
trailers to launch at sunrise. Here

Centralia's colliery still smolders like
fields of burning cane. The trees

stand dead but don't fall.
Veins in the Gulf will swell, too,

carrying grayed-out swirls—ghosts—
to greed's unbroken refrain.

Creation

From the beginning we knew You
Were a mud dauber, that we'd

Have to look for You under the eaves,
That You'd be so intent on your crude

Grottoes You wouldn't perceive our scrutiny,
And, of course, later You would

Come spiraling down stinger first,
Your inadequate warning so much like

Everything we make: an idle hum,
An idle motor, softer than the gentle

Hummingbird who passes by Your
Clay cells in search of something blue,

Something unambiguous, whose flames
Destroy, destroy and keep us warm.

The Dirty Side of the Storm

Death just misses you, its well-defined
eye and taut rotation land on
someone else. No need to study the sky

for signs or watch the cows—
not with satellite loops, infrared
imagery, reconnaissance flights shrinking

the orange cones of uncertainty.
If it makes you feel better, go ahead
and push pins through a brittle chart.

Your coordinates square neatly east
of the worst wind shear, lightning
strikes, and bursts of air.

All convection steers clear
of your splattered doorframe.
The Red Cross mobilizes elsewhere.

Take a good look at those oak roots
from a calm doorstep and wait.
The sadness is a surge carrying

all its debris back to you, a flood
that shoves clods of ants and snakes
through your walls and then

sits in your house for days and days.
This is the dirty side of the storm.
Would that Death had blown straight through.

The Discipline of Nonfulfillment

for and after Margaret A. Farley

Eastertide, Margaret, and all
That we've given up comes back
To us at once, chicken and

Sausage gumbo, twelve-packs of Dixie,
Picayunes, and the man-god builder
Of trawl boards who frees bird dogs

And coons from steel jaws.
At once the humid air rolls back
And northern light pours through.

Girls in pastel dresses spin, petals
To relieve pink azaleas
Of carrying the day

On their own. A crowded
Sea of greens, innocent water
Wedged by shorn banks below.

Eastertide, Margaret, and *tide*
Means something different here,
But wouldn't you say it's the same

Sweeping abundance overtaking
Shoals and inlets, joining lake and bay,
Drowning everything in between?

Don't answer. I'll focus on some small
Thing, a blue heron lifting from brown stubble,
Light off bleached barnacles, helicopter blades

Beating the marsh into submission.
No action hero will rappel down
In camouflage or lab white

To sew together the last scraps
Of duckweed and spoil, like *the*
Discipline of nonfulfillment

You offered from the pulpit
Years ago, as if you were explaining
The abbreviated life of dogs

To children, laying a still,
Furry body down in its damp
Space and closing up the hole.

Prasada

Semi-submersible Lord,
we withdraw from the crystalline
beaches and heavy tides where cattle

once trod and cross over
to your side, to your jackup
altars, to your subsea trees, to your

black blood relics pumping around us.
On the seventh day, we are still working.
On the eighth day, we go home

to scattered brick vaults, church bells
ringing against a crude sky.
Citrus trees strewn by the hundreds

across the roadway, fruit
bobbing in flooded barrooms.
All our lives we have worshiped

the wrong gods. Hot-tempered water
and summer air collude
to press their dominance into us.

Strangers Hotel

What happened to the wide-verandaed
Strangers Hotel, bold letters

like a black headline on white cedar siding?
What news it would be for an exile—

as if monks slid the latches, opening shuttered
doors onto bourbon-dark carpets

and deep oak trim. To lean out
a second-floor window—half in

shade, a motionless cloud of egrets and
elephant ears on the *batture*—

almost home, but not yet, deep
in swamp and the constancy of *other*.

Bayou Lafourche

It seems laid like rails, without acquaintance,
    old dog impervious to floorboards.

Whatever leaving took place, the quandary
    of rich sediment unbraiding itself—

the River disentangled, one lashing
    current at a time, swerving toward South Pass—

first, reprieve, then that trickle of instinct:
    What was once nearby, closer than skin, is

not gone, but diminished, dissolved, and
    into that space, mourning, but before—

an undertow indistinguishable
    from desire, laying its full length

on the body so, partnered, it can sleep.
    And then the bayou moves on moving on,

like the Yellow Dog on a tight schedule,
    a steel bridge across its brow, hardheads

and dead cattle swirling, somewhat slowly,
    toward the washtub misnamed *Gulf*.

Fais Do-Do

A green heron pulls the sky behind it
like a zipper. Sharp rows

of clouds fold into themselves, erasing
the framed blue tide.

Barrier islands disappear into
the Gulf's gray mouth.

Everywhere something strives to overtake something else:
Grass over a mound of fill dirt, ants over grass,

the rough shading of rust between rows
of sheet metal frustrating the sky.

Boats breast up three deep in every slip,
and, as soon docked, are waved away.

The only music's crickets and lapping,
happy bullfrogs on slick logs.

A rustling skirt of palmettos
around the roots of a modest oak

that appear after hard rain. A fiddle,
or idling motor, moves away.

Go to sleep. God will come
in an extended cab for all of us:

the children, the dogs, the poets.
That old Adversary, the Gulf,

our succoring Mother, having given
everything, will carry the whole of us away.

Ordinary Time

When the world was beginning to begin,
a noisy, cosmic battle flashed between
a lightning bolt and a single speck of mud.

Or there was silence.
Or the sound of sea-doors shutting.
Or another postulant that keeps us awake.

Now the sea is under the house,
across roads, covering marsh,
silted depths where hardheads crowd dark grasses.

In Ordinary Time one theory follows another.
They fold together like pleats on a gray wool skirt,
children counted like beads into pews.

My first loves are knives and fire
because they are dangerous and beautiful.
Dangerous meaning anything can happen.

Beautiful that something already has.
The beginning of a flame,
the end of a match.

Abraham holds a knife to a boy's throat
and kindles fire beneath him.
What is the boy's name?

To what woman was he born?
This end was not his end.
He walked down the mountain

without mortification and with
a god who would not be named.

    Levees are a river's burnt
offerings—charming, but inconsequential.
When the floodwaters rise, the luggers

disappear like embers. Weirs,
relieved of responsibility,
stagger in a jumbled second line.

Rain sounds like rain anywhere,
a deluge in Chauvin is a deluge in Bangladesh.
A bare foot in a swollen ditch.

A thumb, cut open, presses
against the altar and turns
to wine in a cup of fired clay.

    Across a white-draped
casket, the thick-tongued
sing the Sanctus

for stars lined up like votives.
The solitary oak beside the cane fields,
a giant fist of roots holding

the ground firm. Branches
reach out from its palm
for me, but I cannot move to climb.

After spring rains, resurrection
fern drapes the hard bark railings.
White-washed crosses gleam like beer cans.

Wharves stand like relics in the rain.

Bully Camp Road

Every mangled, rusty hood reads "CLOSE!"
In white grease print, as if something might
Escape, like a mad dog through a screen door

Or Freon-charged air from a struggling
Window unit in Cocodrie mid-
July, from this junkyard of car shells

Turtle-stacked along a sagging chain-link fence.
A curl-tip of blackberry springs up
From a chrome gear shift, commanding

What's left of this pickup's interior:
Seat rails, speaker wires, steering column,
A Fritos bag and a few flakes of glass

From the mosaic bubble of punched-
Out windshield. Its bottle-green leaves against
The hollowed dash make it look a little

Lost, a little upstream. Don't think *hope*, for
God's sake. Think *vulnerable*. Think of that day
In kindergarten, telling the teacher—

She so pleased with fifteen etched Christmas cards—
Mama got them from the back of some drawer.
Think how complicated *truth* became.

Most of these jalopies are picked clean
To their Detroit bones: not a rearview
To be had, not a taillight to follow

Down a swamp road. And this road is a long
One, all caked dust and oyster shells, past
The house of a boy who set off a shot-

Gun under his head, so that his tongue,
I'm sure, was the first to go, a collage
Of rote recitals, blunders, and dreams.

Echoes endure, chalky dust quiets,
Almost settles, like this passenger cage,
Razed to a mound of glinting red powder.

Ghost Trees

Pointe Aux Chênes, LA

Toward season's end when butterfly trawls spill
purple-eyed shrimp, and a cool north wind scatters
mosquitoes across the bay—moon's running,

crabs are fat, blowfish surface with hardheads
and flounder like minnows to a lantern—under
a giant moon like this you can see ghost trees,

a stark statuary across the marsh. You'd think some
gravedigger tended these lacy roots, trimmed the grass,
and whitewashed the skin of their contorted branches.

(If live oaks walked, you might guess these looked back
and were quicklimed to their lonely, twisted spots.)
As if through a peephole frame, you see the past—

a ridge of green smoke, the vestige of fresh
water through the *chêniére*—dissolve in the haze.
Salt has blanched the bark stone-smooth—no olive-

colored leaves hanging like lures—the ghost trees hold
only the memory of solid ground, their coiled roots
braid nothing but brackish water and air. Storms

can't challenge this specter—frozen in agony
or ecstasy, who knows which, and what does it matter
when their shining bodies keep forking the darkness?

Pushing the Channel

The landscape's only black velvet
and mauve sky. Just a chinstrap of a moon.

Come dusk greenhead horseflies gnaw at your back.
Mosquitoes lighting on your raw neck and arms

are easier to ignore. When the current's
running, shrimp skim right off the top. They come up

pretty clean, a few squid, flounder, and soft-
shelled crab. An orange ember

pins the sepia figure on another
trawl boat, green and red lights running.

Two good pushes fill your chests. Pick them clean,
and stay on the deep parts of the channel.

Catching the Bridge

Along the *batture* cars squat, windows down,
Their drivers' arms slung across side mirrors.

Sorry, I caught the bridge, an easy white lie
Until we get held up for true.

It's sweltering, and the tug just crawls.
Reluctant pulleys yank the pontoon open, all

A matter of reverse effort. A huge
Barge muscles water up the murky

Bayou. Shotgun shacks flash across the highway,
Like the flattened tombstones they might become.

Heat rises off asphalt, an afterthought.
Crackling oyster shells under rubber,

A distantly burning field. That tender's
Missing an arm, his short sleeve, a lost glove.

Something's missing here, too. Racing from one
Bank of the narrow bayou to the other

And back again to outrun—an absence?
A satin train spreads behind the boat,

Floats between the banks. Like an oak church
Door snagging a lace ribbon, the bridge closes

On the wake no one can touch, and the black-
And-white bars free us for where we mean to go.

Sunrise

The first three-floor building in lower Lafourche—
Lady of the Sea—landed like *Apollo*
11: a new Otis, paved parking, halogen
Security lights. The old blue one swam in its shadow:
Strung double-wides, wooden stairs,
An ER ramp where in the red glare
From the Rose Bowl I had my first smoke.

In New York I worked on the fifty-seventh floor.
Every morning I imagined the ride up was
The sluggish moment of dying, the snug room
Smaller, soaring, me stuck with people
I didn't know, their faces distant and smoldering.
Everyone I did know had a walk-up or a doorman.
We were never on the ground but stared intently

At blinds raised a few yards from our windows. Today
I woke up eight stories above Houston. Downtown,
A thick clump of trees in a pasture, what was once
A pasture, and what in my mind are forty arpents
Behind our house. When the levees gave,
Alligators waited it out in our high-rise backyard,
All three inches above sea level.

Look how the fog paves my view. Even indoors
There's the marshy smell of land not really land,
Land the new light is shoring up, land in love
With these absurd buildings bobbing on
Its surface. If I jumped, the haze might net
Me the way a trawl would. The pavement would certainly
Give way, sensing how much swamp I really am.

Reburial at Sea

Leeville Cemetery, LA

They must have heard it coming—
the relentless marsh water
throwing itself against their vaults,
salt-heavy and exhausted, day
after day, the old bricks
warmed in the noon sun.
It must have sounded like regret, like
a bunkmate's throaty breathing
getting louder and closer
as the deckhands roll from sleep.
It must have set the marsh struggling,
high tide's long, muddy arms
that lift bodies into a bath
or onto the quilted Gulf.
It must have kept them company,
the persistent lapping, the slow rock down—
when one holds still, the world's
rough motions calm into shining ripples.
They must have been comforted
that change is possible for the dead.

Hard Rain

A day I mistake bright sun for clarity.
Grass blades shine under gabardine party
dresses: azalea and bougainvillea.

A vague moon floats like a nun
in the sky's crowded playground. I
mistake bright sun for clarity. I mistake

button bush and water lily for happiness.
I mistake old love for absence,
the clamor of grackles for rancor.

Cane trucks waddle down the highway.
Bagasse cliffs and piles of cut cane orient
a field of stubble. I mistake grinding

time for closure. Thunder comes
down like a maul, and then hard rain
that stings cheeks and forearms,

slams every thought and action closed,
beats the world with metal sheets—
cars pulled over on shoulders,

wipers doused, headlights filled—and is
lost in the steam off the asphalt's surface.
It collects in the swales, in the canebrakes,

under the crossings, in root beds, in
my jeans, on the U-turned petals of irises,
in the oily bowls of magnolias,

in the burnished leaves of crotons,
the barrel chests of live oaks, and for
a moment as ballast in my hands.

Psalm at High Tide

Rain on the river's vinyl surface:
water that glitters,
water that hardly moves,
its branches witness to trees,
to fronds, leaves, crab floats, pilings,
shopping carts, appliances—
the divine earth takes everything
in its wounded side
and gives back wholeness.
It bears the huddled profane
and endures the soaking
venerated in its wild swirls—
this river fixed with wooden weirs,
radiant in misshapen glory.

Returning

Robins drunk on the tiny fruit
Of sabal palms

And hummingbirds popping
Against hibiscus

Empty statues white as gardenia
Bird wings that lace

The trees' crossed branches and
Wide translucent leaves

Snakes' geometric patterns stretched
Between warm rows

Of sawgrass—nothing to fear
And at the center

A grand oak seems to twist
Reaching one branch

Toward the south and arching
Another toward the north

And another reaching its many
Tributaries straight up

The ashy moss cuffing them
With woven bracelets

The garden is very small
Its pond not very deep

And around it a wall
Of coquina

High as a great banana tree
Or as two tall men

Before they get old
Slick orange

Lichen and yellow jasmine
Appear to confine

The garden, its pond, and the birds
It seems to be

Such a small place
Such a lonely place

It seems no one could be happy
There in the cell with snakes

And poisonous flowers
And the eerie silence

At night the boughs of the grand oak
Utterly still

Mosquitoes dimpling black water
Scale the wall. Get back in.

Faith in Florida

First month in Florida I couldn't get used
to the lizards scuttling across my driveway

and my garden, startling me in my kitchen,
swiping their tails in determined retreat.

Then I decided they were manifestations
of divine presence—now we get on fine.

I would even say they comfort me.
Their thrashing through the leaves sounds like wings

beating into sudden flight. My father,
on the gray porch of the house on Crescent

Boulevard, the house where he was born,
had me talking to lizards when I was five

or so. *Lizard, lizard, show me your penny,*
and their throats opened to bright red discs.

It was like magic. He spoke the words again,
and again they obeyed, blasting their round red

trumpets. (My grandmother told me alligators
swam in her ivy sea to keep me on the steps.)

Without my father around, I have to conjure
and believe my own stories, perhaps as he

learned to do without her, fiercely call *proof*
the signs we know have been there all along.

No-Name Storm

The peacock that for months roamed
the green belt on River and Kenneth

blew over from the zoo without mention
like the urban homeless perched

on the landmarks of our commutes, not
on platforms and doorways but on pine trees

and jacaranda—what we might acquaint
in ourselves divorced by the drive—

our morning-coffee travel cups, sidelong glances
over pursed, slurping lips as if cobalt plumes

and a fan of eyes were just another line
of palm trees, another plodding timeline.

The nameless storm brooded over the Gulf,
sucking water from inlets and rivers—

soggy frogs swapping duck calls,
banana leaves ripped to streamers,

ants clumped on the surface of rising
water, a rebellious yellow sky

against our faces like a darkened mirror,
an alchemized image no longer discernible,

only the plaintive scream of the peacock,
its unintelligible, unpronounceable refrain.

To the Landlady

On Sundays you hang your rugs out on the fence
Between my house and yours, or between your big house
And your *smaller* one, where I live, exist, lease . . .

I try to imagine them as prayer mats,
Your bourgeois house an ashram full of chanting
Seekers, "The mind is a Trickster. Free the mind."
But in the end they are only ugly bath mats.

Like a vulture in Spandex, you've circled
Your John Deere, glared at my guests,
Measured the time the paper sat in the drive
Till I grabbed my ripped-up robe and retrieved it.

Compassion is like heartburn. It hits you
Suddenly and then you never forget.
Or it doesn't hit you and you never
Think about it seizing you, ever.

I have prayed for it, looked into the welled
Eyes of my golden retriever, who seems
To have supply in abundance for me.
O Landlady, why do you tick me off so?

At least you are female or that word "lord"
Would come in, confusing me with its claims
Of divinity. You can't *lady* it over me,

Or can you? Lord, Lord, we should own nothing,
Like You, God, who has given all away—

Formica

My uncle offers a can of "coffee"
at seven in the morning as he

disappears into his mint green truck—
the lakes he fished gather

tupelos and moss thick as his heart—
disguising its will as his, crickets

and the pop of the float reminding him
of the world's insistent presence, though

by seven he's done fishing, long done,
just driving into clouds of oyster dust—

leaving us to Green Stamp coffee cups,
cuccidata, iced pink and white,

from fat figs in her side yard, whites
on a clothesline, cats eating from pie pans

on the car hood, on the boat trailer,
the final metal snap like a crystal

dinner bell, or what she imagines a dinner
bell would sound like, or a baby's voice.

In the photograph she slings an arm
like a sailor across her sister's shoulder.

They have the Pop-Rouge-and-Moon-pie
grins of being-in-love. The itinerant photographer

maybe missing that, as they did maybe,
the multiplicities of romance. *How can*

those young girls pull down their step-ins
for a man? It's bad enough . . . she said, and

Get down and have some coffee, cher.
Here inside the checkered floor,

glass-paned cabinets, you can see what
you need right inside, no lost time

on the green-spackled Formica,
chrome-wrapped table, doilies,

everything in easy reach—lighten,
sweeten, stir, smell, savor, and

drink, *Cher, you can tell me,* wiped by a clean
towel with a crocheted and consecrated lip.

Undertaking History

A pink-taffeta-ball-gown-and-bourbon
sky, gaslights twirling like pendants in glass.

Only cane trucks turn russet in autumn,
against the power station's transformers,

against the strung fire of burning cane,
smoke that slices the season to stubble.

A silver pirogue on Petit Caillou,
Fan's claret wrist draped over the rudder,

a blunted cigarette bobbing from his
Brandoesque bottom lip. Sudden cypress knees

and the black water that recalls their shapes,
evergreens on his shoulders like a mantle.

He's cooling his forehead, cap tipped back,
scanning the tree line, brooding, above time.

Nine a.m. on a Saturday and he's
learning, squaring the twenty-two between

the bars, resting the sight between a surprised
pig's eyes and squeezing, while the beer-drinking

fathers and uncles lean against the cage,
the crown of his ten-year-old head uncovered.

Christmas at Coushatta

There's a push at the blackjack table,
a new dealer waiting in the wings,

her Santa-suit lips bleeding into smile
lines, origins forgotten, a blue wisp

dancing above someone's Pall-Mall and
old-fashioned, old people tethered to slots,

bells above the grinding wheels of walkers
on loud carpet beneath the mistletoe.

What your hand finds to throw, throw
with all your might. Buy the back, get in

past the inconceivable wager, past
the vinyl-roped tables. And although

the neon halos look like idols,
no one looks up from the floor. Some faith

thrives at green felt altars,
at every congregated table, and

except for the shining poinsettias,
it might be any other day.

In the end you lean into the wrought
iron cages and cash out, join

the mourners in the street or rejoice
with the lucky on the trembling main deck.

Behind you the Yuletide squares spin.
The ball hops first to red, then green, then black.

Millennial Birthday

My twenty-first my dad took me to Vegas
To play blackjack into dawn, swearing
we'd quit, then someone brings free seven-

And-sevens and a pack of Marlboro
Lights on a cork tray of swizzle sticks
And gold embossed napkins and how,

You think, could you have doubted
The abundance of the world, as
You tap the table for another card.

      And that's a *good* day—
After you stop going to therapy,
Which is, after all, strategy sessions

For winning the game you're
Trying to quit. A good day
Is walking the dog beside the river,

When, among palmettos and
Ibises, I look squarely at the stiff
Red-tail knotted in the Kash n' Karry bag.

There's the osprey all alone
At the top of the spindly bald cypress,
And somehow I at once

Feel at home and at some other
Point, not faraway, but where,
In my memory, everything

Was bigger, the legs of the dining room
Table thick as these oak trees,
Shaggy, hard and magisterial.

I have lived where green things live
All year long and where snow becomes
The only color beside dull and gray and hard.

Now I live where buzzards winter.
In the mornings they flare their opera capes
And until night I must perform.

Conveyance

For seven days I held a rosary's ivory
beads, scattered river stones across
the foamy cuffs of waves.

Seven years Perma-Seal kept me from washing
his bones in wine, hanging them from oaks, untangling
time. *Just as the body is dead*

Without the spirit, so is faith apart
from works. Everything mildews and goes
to dust. You can't take it with you,

Nor can you leave it behind. "My father makes
files," I'd have said as a child. A novelist and
a magician, he numbered the dead

And the just-born like cities. When he signed
his name to a page, the words marched across
the world like machines into history.

Years later, when I opened the boxes,
the pages softened like clay. All the decay
of people who lived and died in his

Excavated city. What you take away
marks a spot by its absence: the green lizard's
thick belly resting on a crossbeam,

Tiny blades of eggshell wedged between tabs
of white-out. One night I laid myself
on a slab beside porcelain

Chemicals. Around me caskets in Ziploc bags.
All night nothing came to take me away.
The man who made trawl boards

Held my shoulders like a priest: *I stayed*
stupid when he died, he said,
my hands open to him

As if they were nets he could mend.
Two horses stood in the radiance
of the fire we built. Box

After box resisted the flames, and my father's
handwriting rose from folder after folder:
Do Not Destroy, they chided. And we chased

Down the scraps that blew away, drove
down the rest with sticks, every
artifact razed. And although

It was Eastertide—the roads long cleared—
up on the roof I could see a few broken strands
of beads, a festive epitaph across tar shingles

Scripted in yellow, purple, and green.
Through damp smolder I read everything
we'd made and all our names.

No Matter What Happens
Everything Will Be All Right

she says at the resolution of almost
every fight, and I hate her for it
although she shakes back at me

my own apokatastatic belief
like drops of water from a frond.
All things work for the good, all manner

of things shall be well. And like the very
thirsty, I can't take in the drench: loners,
hand-wringers, misanthropes, heroes

alike will close their eyes and be taken up.
But for me alone there will be purgatory:
long nights late in Lafitte's Blacksmith's

Shop, dank and smoky. Crude flambeaux
with no mercy, fearless river rats skulking
along the bared *bousillage*, illusory

threads of slow-moving water thrown
against the grotto's plaster walls. Under my feet,
the slosh and buckle of dammed water.

I'll lie in button-fly jeans and no shirt
and collect lost prospects on cave floors.
As land disappears from the grasp

of shore trees, erosion like a tennis match
of no serves returned, I watch love
empty into the river, silt from under me,

me alone in purgatory, the rest of creation
swimming into particles of pure light,
the rest of creation all illumined and all right.

The Sinking of the *Southern Belle*

From the *batture* we watched her go down,
another liturgical rite of the Lost Cause,
another initiation, repression, submersion.
We turned loose her demitasse, her debutante,

her demure, her defer, her deny, her desist.
A pool of pancake, of pretense, of proper
preference, concession, primness in oily reds,
whites and blues off the shore. One flood, one storm,

one wake-up call too many sent her down.
Or would that last cupped white glove really
retire below the waves? Could she rise

the morning after? Her last manipulative,
domineering deferential act of obeisance
was to leave us a racy hem of lace bow.

Skinned

After two weeks, my skin returns.
The rain on the outside
and the rain on the inside are discrete.

I miss the color red
on the horizon and over my eyes.
I miss the pooled water on the sill

that someone has sopped
with a sponge left within
reach of the sink.

I miss sap and wind
moving through me.
I miss the agony of others.

I miss oak branches most:
those saluting the sky
and those laid out on mottled grass.

The Pomegranate

On the tray is a pomegranate and
a pot of decaf. Room service.

Blue Oxford tails
wriggle beneath a rough sweater.

See, this is not desire.
This is the snake taunting.

I won't be able to—I don't know you.
Clever boy, he gets his own pun.

Night air sags over the cricket's
pauses as if stunned

by the sudden inconsequence.
Look on from the banks:

a clump of turtles on a half-submerged
log, sunning themselves. They

do not want the dark water.
They leave the clammy bank to us.

Everywhere are oaks, impervious
to Spanish moss, resurrection fern,

crested woodpeckers. Hundreds
of cypress engendering hundreds

of knees fall over into the river.
A long time ago someone said

knowledge and someone else
wisdom, but that voice

was so lilting and quiet,
the way two women talk

in a garden, and the white lilies
lift their trumpets to listen.

After Theism

The day spreads like land below sea level
At four a.m. and into dawn—

Bald cypresses point to a cloudless wide sky.
There is nothing there and no measure for

How faraway *there* is.

An Act of Mercy

Justice is what keeps us awake at night,
Its abundance or its lamentable absence.

Regret rests well, like a dog that hogs the bed.
Each way we turn, he presses against us,

Our legs pinned to the sheets. Endless dissections,
Every gesture splayed and stuck to the cork.

Love heals, my dear friend said in the bar.
She has twenty years on me and better know.

Loves are as countless as herbs and who knows
When to pick what for what ailment?

I don't feel comfortable in my skin, my lover
Cries, unmoved to crawl over into mine.

We are all looking for a forward-motion—
Only life—then headlights half-stab our eyes.

What an act of mercy it would be
To set judgment aside like a flat stone,

Reach back for each sin and find a spring,
Blue and gelatinous, cool aloe to the touch.

Sand

Fine as baby powder somewhere
but not here

Here coarse and brown as pine cones
or blackberry thorns

And just as stubborn
How many times

Can I knock my feet
against the threshold

Shake my fingers through my hair
And still I find

A few specks clinging
to my ears

Each repeating, *I am the whole world*
and I tip the scales before you

Gaze

When I consider Your thereness
    and Your absence, I stare,
      like a young man new

To the art of sidelong
    glances, who stops mid-step
      to turn and gawk at a backside

Passing, or like gazing upon wrought iron,
    both constant and yielding:
      balconies where the sleepless

Stretch and sigh, where the carnal
    dangle golden beads
      like long tongues above

The crowd; shielding banisters
    holding up from down;
      fire screens branding light

With flourishes and synapses,
    spaces for passion, warmth,
      and rain-soaked ashes.

White Clover

Stop knotting garlands out of them
and let them grow

in the outfield where their scrolls gather,
in pastures where they sit like lotuses

among the lucky three-lobed
disfavored and alive

unlike the four-leafs
hundreds dried and languishing

in old books and pierced to cork.
Let them stand in the water-logged

air of summer and the irrelevance
of winter and their shape,

something like an open eyeball
to the sun, should be a reminder

of something, something forgotten,
something that persists despite

any effort of the mind and grows
in the outfields in green-flecked knots.

Tinsel

They lie rather disgraced along the shoreline,
shorn of their flocking and tinsel, a bulkhead
of expedience, sacred and secular.

Strange ornaments now grace fir and pine:
icicles of tar, a garland of brown foam.
They exhale the voices of their former rooms:

getting, getting, getting, and, of course, giving
a dead tree to save the dead marsh, which has
atoned for all it can, striped with canals

and gasping at the consuming Gulf.
More than a cupful it has drunk, holding
ashen oaks like gnarled tapers to the ground.

On New Year's, we hurl our righteous trees
on the city truck. Even the treacherous Gulf
can't wash apostasy off their branches.

The Boat Shed

Long after the salvage,
the boat shed covers the shadowed tide,
feeling the hull inside its shiplap
like a ghost limb, like a thought

inside a dream. So we named
the bar after its falling roof
and split sides, a crumbling
shelter for all we've lost—

rusty bow a few steps
from the door and a varnished
wheel running wild toward
closing time—these shells

in the parking lot, more like white stones
in a field keeping watch.

The Morning After the Parade
Has Passed

Beneath a half-moon's edge
    littered with frass,
Broken beads hang from trees like moss
On the neutral ground, and winds
    shake palm fronds into
    waves that never fall.

Live oak roots sprawl like the night's
Lost drunks or like lovers entwined in sleep.
    Enter churning street cleaners
Whispering *au revoir*—or is it *aubade*,
But there has been no lovemaking—
    only dawn snuffing the lights
    of absent flambeaux.

Decreation

We must be rooted in the absence of a place.
—SIMONE WEIL

1.

On this fork of sandbagged and bunkered beach,
    plumes of oyster grass attend open water
and oil rigs blot the horizon. Between

every two, one slightly smaller fades, more distant,
    a pen stroke blending heaven and the gray
Gulf of Earth. Mercurial tides contend

with offshore wind, turn deep charcoal, and recede.
Pink clouds drift awkwardly like erasures.

A hand's width above the waves, a pelican,
    plumb with mullet below, defies these signs.
Trawlers lift their wings in egress: white-

bellied crabs, handfuls of marsh pulled apart
    and falling, like rewinding light, into
the wide mouth of an early dusk.

A driven reed blown back into the sand,
into the rough roots and gray-black surf.

2.

Up the bayou, past smoldering cane fields
    burnt to their elements, is a crossing where
tankers drag three engines backwards

down the tracks—the wheels, groaning objections,
    move where they don't want to go—Union
Pacific, Equity—past the citadel of the refinery,

dim orange in Convent's eternal flame.
Rusty points of cypress waver in the foreground.

3.

From the sky the marsh rises like moldy velour,
    like swatches of work shirts and dungarees
floating in an oil-slicked wash. Light poles

march off into water. Lakes take over
    lakes and scant arpents in between. Pastures,
ant mounds, and crawfish holes foam green

on the Gulf's surface
like thick lather around a bathing body.

4.

The fishermen anchor at Leeville's sunken graves,
    cast their lures among broken crypts
that stagger down the shoal like

brass-plated divers. Cement crosses shoulder
    waves and wide-mouthed roofs pull in
a continuous salt spray.

As if the dead were neither dead nor living,
the living land speckled trout among their empty tombs.

If I could dive headlong into the brackish
    water, a pelican after
a fish. If I could forget the sand, this wax

myrtle, before they fold back behind
    the doors of the water, behind the *forest
primeval*, the shrouded oaks

watching from their ridge. Empty as coat stands.
Orange and lemon groves sting the air thick with oils.

5.

I floated above the priest's head and sat
    on the marble cornice of a fat Roman
column in the nave of Sacred Heart.

Like rain on pavement all over the world,
    we were gray, but stone gray, immovable,
unlike the spongy swamp beneath our feet. And hand bells

cut like filament, just as translucent
and magical. Tie fishing line to anything,

tug on it, and things move at your command.
  Corpus Christi. One flesh but two spirits
churning like magnets. We cannot have

what we most want because wanting itself holds us back,
  longing occupies the space of our being,
the oceanic space before we were cut free.

The cord itself is a vapor from the sea.
A past tenant's portrait hanging in the hall.

6.
If only I could give the land my body—
  Dig and water fills the pit,
not even a foothold before it brims.

Someone will lay a plaster vault for me to ride,
  like long boxes children pull down flooded roads.
In my plaster boat I'll ride Gulf shores

till I vanish like a rig in the sun.
If only the land would take me now,

I would lie against the marsh grass and sink,
  muck enfolding me, and welcome the eroding Gulf—
handful by handful, carrying us away.

Who could have known how much the land wants the water,
    to be the water, to forget? We carve
and sign and plaster our impressions.

But then there will be no names, no
fierce grip of the undertow along the pier

or hiss of barnacles' anxious breathing.
    I'll imagine us seated at a crab boil,
potatoes and onions steaming, orange

and blue crabs over orange and blue propane,
    another Friday in Lent, newspaper and lemon
halves, cayenne stinging our nail beds. See,

a fog rests over the marshland, everything
water, nothing outside grace and gray chaos.

Eulogy

We lay out our wetlands
    on a Wednesday

A wastebasket of rosaries
    on a table

It merely looks asleep
    its brown lids peaceful

Silent waterbirds and all
    kinds of insects gone

We gather to smoke in the kitchen:
    all the speckled trout it gave up

All those white shrimp and oysters
    big as a man's hand

Pirogue races on the bayou
    the Blessing of the Fleet

Father Comeaux
    cussing a blue streak

Mosquitoes keep getting bigger
    and blacker

Moving farther up the road—
    Old Lady Ducos

Can remember the days
    before the rigs

Back when you put somebody away
    you used to have to dig

A Future with Hope

In threads of moss and potato vines,
    grimy sidewalks, chain-link fence,
a convincing dampness, on leaves,
on roots, under the eaves of houses.

Branches bar the black-oak sky.
    Crows and grackles bear what
yellow light there is. Between
wrought iron gates, a slight wind.

Leave hope there where it belongs,
    on the other side of the levee
where later it can be found easily,
its weight, bread crusts on water.

But here in the middle,
    between the slow river
and cypress, stands a single blue
heron, barely moving. Watch.

Poem Found

New Orleans, September 2005

. . . And God said, "Let there be a dome in the midst
of the waters" and into the dome God put

the poor, the addicts, the blind, and the oppressed.
God put the unsightly sick and the crying young

into the dome and the dry land did not appear.
And God allowed those who favored themselves

born in God's image to take dominion over
the dome and everything that creeped within it

and made them to walk to and fro above it
in their jumbo planes and in their copy rooms

and in their conference halls. And then
God brooded over the dome and its multitudes

and God saw God's own likeness in the shattered
tiles and the sweltering heat and the polluted rain.

God saw everything and chose to make it very good.
God held the dome up to the light

like an open locket and in every manner called
the others to look inside and those who saw

rested on that day and those who didn't
went to and fro and walked up and down

the marsh until the loosened silt gave way
to a void, and darkness covered the faces with deep sleep.

NOTES

"Prasada" (a sacred food offering; Sanskrit, "grace") includes
    altered lines from Louise Glück's "The Reproach."

A *fais do-do* ("go to sleep") is an event, a traditional Cajun dance,
    named for the practice of putting children to bed in the
    dance hall.

"Sunrise" is for Cynthia Macdonald.

"Returning" is for Jeff Klepfer.

"Conveyance" quotes James 2:26.

Bousillage ("No Matter What Happens Everything Will Be All
    Right") is a mixture of mud and Spanish moss used as mor-
    tar or insulation in the construction of traditional Cajun
    houses.

"The Sinking of the *Southern Belle*" is for Dahn Dean Gandell.

"Sand" echoes Wisdom 11:22.